MINNESOTA
WILD

BY CHRÖS MCDOUGALL

Book design by Maggie Villaume
Cover design by Maggie Villaume

Photographs ©: Stacy Bengs/AP Images, cover; Alex Gallardo/AP Images, 4–5, 7, 9; Nick Wosika/Icon Sportswire, 10–11; Ed Andrieski/AP Images, 12–13; Fred Jewell/AP Images, 15; Tom Olmscheid/AP Images, 16; David Zalubowski/AP Images, 18–19, 21; Robin Alam/Icon Sportswire, 23; Brett Holmes/Icon Sportswire, 24–25, 28–29; Dustin Bradford/Icon Sportswire, 27

Press Box Books, an imprint of Press Room Editions.

ISBN
978-1-63494-492-2 (library bound)
978-1-63494-518-9 (paperback)
978-1-63494-569-1 (epub)
978-1-63494-544-8 (hosted ebook)

Library of Congress Control Number: 2022902271

Distributed by North Star Editions, Inc.
2297 Waters Drive
Mendota Heights, MN 55120
www.northstareditions.com

Printed in the United States of America
082022

ABOUT THE AUTHOR

Chrös McDougall is a sportswriter and author from the Twin Cities in Minnesota. Growing up he spent many cold winter nights playing outdoor hockey at a local rink. These days, he spends more time writing about sports from his home in Minneapolis, where he lives with his wife, two kids, and an energetic boxer named Eira.

TABLE OF CONTENTS

1

Kirill Kaprizov skates with the puck during his first NHL game.

A THRILLING
START

Kirill Kaprizov had never played in a hockey game quite like this one. On January 14, 2021, Kaprizov made his debut with the Minnesota Wild. However, the only cheers came from a loudspeaker. Due to the COVID-19 pandemic, most arenas weren't allowing fans to attend games. The pandemic had also forced the

National Hockey League (NHL) to shorten its season.

Wild fans had spent years waiting for Kaprizov. The team selected him in the 2015 draft. At the time, Kaprizov was only 18 years old. But the talented left winger remained in his native Russia for five more years. During that time, he won an Olympic gold medal. He also became a star in Russia's top hockey league. Finally, at age 23, he stepped onto the ice in a Wild sweater.

Minnesota opened the season on the road against the Los Angeles Kings. Late in the first period, Kaprizov set up Wild defenseman Jonas Brodin for the game's first goal. However, the Kings scored

Jonas Brodin (25) celebrates with teammates after scoring against the Los Angeles Kings.

the next three. Entering the third period, Minnesota needed a spark. Kaprizov provided it. He earned another assist on Victor Rask's goal. Six minutes later, Wild forward Marcus Foligno scored to tie the game.

With 80 seconds left in overtime, the Kings prepared to launch another attack. Instead, a weak pass left them exposed. Kaprizov picked up the puck at the Kings' blue line. It was a breakaway!

The rookie skated toward Kings goalie Jonathan Quick. Kaprizov made a move to the left. Then he slipped the puck past Quick and into the net. Kaprizov's first NHL goal was also a game-winner.

CAPTAIN SPURG

Minnesota celebrated another new beginning against the Kings. The game marked Jared Spurgeon's first as team captain. It continued his remarkable rise. No team selected the defenseman in the 2010 draft. He stood just 5-foot-9. Many believed he was too small for the NHL. But he got an invite to the Wild's training camp. Spurgeon made his NHL debut that November. Before long, he was one of the team's best players.

Kaprizov scores in overtime during his debut with the Minnesota Wild. He became only the third player ever to score in overtime in his first NHL game.

It was a thrilling start to his career. For Minnesota fans, Kaprizov was already showing that he was worth the wait.

KIRILL KAPRIZOV

Few hockey fans had heard the name Kirill Kaprizov before the 2015 NHL draft. Teams selected 134 players before the Wild grabbed Kaprizov in the fifth round. But by the time he finally arrived in Minnesota in 2020, he was already a star.

Kaprizov turned pro as a teenager in his native Russia. The winger soon emerged as an elite offensive player. Russia named him to its 2018 Olympic team. Kaprizov was just 20 years old. With a slap shot, he scored the overtime winner in the gold-medal game. He kept up the offense in Russia's top hockey league. No player scored more goals than Kaprizov in 2018–19 and 2019–20. By then, though, Wild fans were getting nervous. They wondered if he would ever come to North America.

He proved worth the wait. Kaprizov joined the Wild in the 2020–21 season. His dynamic playmaking ability stood out. Kaprizov led all Wild players in goals. He tied for second in assists. It was little surprise when he won the Calder Trophy as the league's top rookie.

2

Craig Hartsburg played 10 seasons for the Minnesota North Stars and served as captain for six of them.

STATE OF HOCKEY

Hockey has a long history in Minnesota. The first organized game in the state took place in 1895. Over the years, hockey thrived in Minnesota at all levels. The sport was popular with youth players, high schoolers, and college students. But for decades, Minnesota didn't have an NHL team.

In 1967, the NHL doubled in size. The league grew from six

teams to twelve. The Minnesota North Stars were one of the new franchises. The team played at the Met Center near Minneapolis. The North Stars enjoyed some successful seasons over the years. In 1981, they made it all the way to the Stanley Cup Final. And in 1991, they reached the Final again.

However, a new owner had bought the North Stars in 1990. He said the team was losing money. So, he moved the franchise to Texas in 1993. The team dropped the word "North" from its name and became known as the Dallas Stars.

Minnesota hockey fans were furious. Their passion for the game was obvious. So, in 1997, the NHL announced it was

Brian Propp of the Minnesota North Stars approaches the goal in a 1991 playoff game.

coming back to Minnesota. The new team would start playing in the 2000–01 season. But before that could happen, there was lots of work to do.

Darby Hendrickson celebrates a goal against the Detroit Red Wings in 2001.

The city of Saint Paul helped build a new arena. Meanwhile, the team needed a name. The franchise settled on the Wild. The name paid tribute to Minnesotans' love for the outdoors. Now all the team needed was players.

The Wild picked winger Marian Gaborik third overall in the 2000 draft. Most other players came from the expansion draft. Among them was center and Minnesota native Darby Hendrickson. The Wild also hired Jacques Lemaire as head coach. Lemaire had won Stanley Cups as both a player and a coach. Finally, on October 11, 2000, the Wild hosted the Philadelphia Flyers. Pro hockey was back in Minnesota.

NEW TRADITIONS

The Wild's arrival brought some new traditions. Before every home game, a youth player skates to center ice and plants a team flag. Also, a special guest leads the crowd in yelling "Let's Play Hockey." Another tradition is the "State of Hockey" anthem. The rousing song is played at all home games.

3

Right winger Richard Park (left) and goalie Manny Fernandez celebrate an overtime win in 2003.

OUT OF THE
WOODS

By the 2002–03 season, the Wild had put together a strong team. At age 20, Marian Gaborik notched his second straight 30-goal season. The team was also embracing coach Jacques Lemaire's defensive system.

With their first winning record in team history, the Wild earned a spot in the playoffs. There, the favored Colorado Avalanche jumped out to a 3–1 series lead. Minnesota never gave up. The Wild won the next two games. That set up a deciding Game 7, which went to overtime. In the extra period, Wild winger Andrew Brunette found an opening. He slipped the puck past superstar goalie Patrick Roy. The stunned Avs could hardly believe it.

Minnesota went down 3–1 in the next round, too. Coming back from that deficit is rare. But the Wild became the first team to do it twice in one postseason. This time they beat the Vancouver Canucks.

However, the dream run ended in the conference finals. The Wild fell to the Mighty Ducks of Anaheim. Even so, the future was looking bright in the State of Hockey.

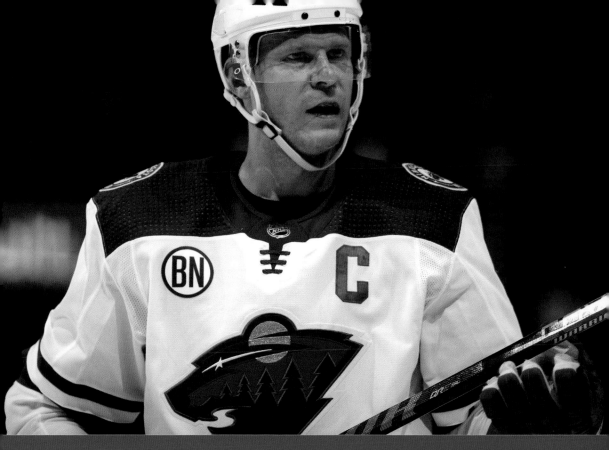

Mikko Koivu played in 1,028 games for the Wild, which is the most in team history.

In November 2005, Mikko Koivu made his debut. Over 15 seasons in Minnesota, the Finnish center set several team records. He was also the Wild's first full-time captain. In December 2007, Gaborik scored five goals in a win over the

New York Rangers. The team also won its first division title that season. But for the second year in a row, the Wild lost in the first round of the playoffs.

By the summer of 2012, the Wild were in need of a change. In 11 seasons, they had made the playoffs just three times. Fans who had supported the team were becoming restless. On July 4, the team

HOCKEY DAY MINNESOTA

The Wild are just one part of Minnesota hockey. No state has more youth players. High school hockey is a way of life for many. Minnesota also has several men's and women's college programs. Since 2007, the sport has been celebrated each year during Hockey Day Minnesota. A local TV station broadcasts games from all levels. Some of the games are even played outside. Hockey Day always ends with a Wild home game.

In 2012, Zach Parise (11) and Ryan Suter (20) both signed 13-year contracts worth $98 million.

made a big announcement. Star players Zach Parise and Ryan Suter had signed with the Wild. An exciting new era was about to begin.

4

In 2018, Zach Parise scored the 341st goal of his career. That was the most ever for a Minnesota-born player.

LET'S GO
WILD

Wild fans were reenergized. Ryan Suter was an ultra-reliable defenseman. Zach Parise, a dangerous left wing, had grown up in Minnesota. His dad, J. P. Parise, had been a beloved North Star. Now Suter and Parise joined Mikko Koivu and several talented young players. The Wild appeared to be on their way.

In 2013, Minnesota lost in the first round of the playoffs.

Then in 2014, the Wild met the Colorado Avalanche in the first round. As in 2003, the series went to seven games. And once again, Game 7 went to overtime. This time, young forward Nino Niederreiter was the star. His goal on an odd-man rush sent the Wild to the next round.

In 2015, Minnesota reached the second round again. This time the Wild upset the St. Louis Blues in the opening series.

THE WINTER CLASSIC

Perhaps no state is more known for outdoor hockey than Minnesota. The Wild had to wait until 2016 to host their first outdoor game. However, what fans really wanted was the Winter Classic. Finally, on New Year's Day 2022, the famous game came to Target Field in Minneapolis. The St. Louis Blues beat the Wild 6–4 in subzero temperatures.

Nino Niederreiter's Game 7 overtime goal came in his first season with the Wild.

However, the Chicago Blackhawks eliminated the Wild every year from 2013 to 2015. And in each of the following three years, the Wild lost in the first round. Fans began to wonder if this group had what it took to make a long playoff run.

Minnesota's playoff streak ended in 2019. But a new one began in 2020.

By then, a new era was beginning in Minnesota. Many of the young players from a few years earlier had been traded away. Koivu left that offseason. The following summer, the team parted ways with Parise and Suter, too.

Management wanted the next generation to take over. That included Russian winger Kirill Kaprizov. He had shined as the NHL's 2021 Rookie of the Year. Joel Eriksson Ek had also emerged as a shutdown center. Meanwhile, defenseman Jared Spurgeon led one of the league's toughest blue lines. Once again, the State of Hockey had reason to be excited about the future.

Jared Spurgeon was named full-time captain in January 2021.

QUICK STATS

FOUNDED: 2000

STANLEY CUP CHAMPIONSHIPS: 0

KEY COACHES:

- Jacques Lemaire (2000–09): 293 wins, 255 losses, 55 ties, 53 overtime losses

- Bruce Boudreau (2016–20): 158 wins, 110 losses, 35 overtime losses

HOME ARENA: Xcel Energy Center (Saint Paul, MN)

MOST CAREER POINTS: Mikko Koivu (709)

MOST CAREER GOALS: Marian Gaborik (219)

MOST CAREER ASSISTS: Mikko Koivu (504)

MOST CAREER SHUTOUTS: Niklas Backstrom (28)

*Stats are accurate through the 2020–21 season.

GLOSSARY

ASSIST
A pass that results in a goal.

CAPTAIN
A team's leader.

DEBUT
First appearance.

DRAFT
An event that allows teams to choose new players coming into the league.

ODD-MAN RUSH
A situation when there are more offensive players than defensive players on an attack.

ROOKIE
A professional athlete in his or her first year of competition.

SLAP SHOT
A shot in which a player winds up and slaps the puck with great force.

WINGER
A forward who typically plays to the side of the net in the offensive zone.

TO LEARN MORE

BOOKS

Duling, Kaitlyn. *Women in Hockey*. Lake Elmo, MN: Focus Readers, 2020.

Graves, Will. *Ultimate NHL Road Trip*. Minneapolis: Abdo Publishing, 2019.

Omoth, Tyler. *A Superfan's Guide to Pro Hockey Teams*. North Mankato, MN: Capstone Press, 2018.

MORE INFORMATION

To learn more about the Minnesota Wild, go to **pressboxbooks.com/AllAccess**.

These links are routinely monitored and updated to provide the most current information available.

INDEX